BUTTERFLY MOMENTS

Sharmini Mendis

tellwell

Tellwell Talent
www.tellwell.ca

ISBN
978-1-77941-831-9 (Hardcover)
978-1-77941-830-2 (Paperback)
978-1-77941-832-6 (eBook)

Table of Contents

In the beginning...

My journey began, into a forest,
Grown from a tiny seed within my mind.
I found a secret place, a kind of exhilaration,
A refuge that was truly mine,

Where teachings from an old master,
Gave shelter and warmth within rhyme.
And even though the present was mesmerising,
I kept sliding back in time,

Captivated by the softness of vintage,
Drawn to Chantilly lace and chandeliers,
Dusty in this new world,
Hiding in my cocoon, I was ready to emerge.

I penned furiously, pondering
This quandary of right or wrong,
The poet's voice strongly echoing
"Seek comfort where you belong."

Your Gifts

My eyes trail onto you,
Chanting ancient prayers.
Palms held together,
A smell of incense wafting through the air,

The skin of your hands; look like parchment.
And as I look down at my own,
I wonder how many times you have prayed for me,
Sitting in this altar all alone,

I listen to the melodious chanting,
Offering loving kindness to your own.
And though life has thrown moments of darkness at you,
It is a tapestry of happiness you have sewn.

I wonder at your many roads in life,
Some leading towards laughter and regret.
How silence has become your strongest ally,
Holding your hand, lest you forget.

Each line on your face tells me a story,
Sometimes through bittersweet tears,
Lessons of life painstakingly written,
In a book bound by love, courage, and fears.

But I can barely hear you,
When you softly speak of yesterday.
Your smile still reflecting the same compassion,
Even though your body is giving up day by day.

The passage of time makes your voice sound so distant,
Now I must squeeze my eyes tightly to hear.
When suddenly, a cold chill runs through my blood once more,
For I realise that you are no longer here.

These days I keep searching for you in my dreams,
Wondering if you can hear me from the stars.
For I regret I couldn't thank you enough for,

Your wisdom,
Your legacy
Your Love.

Hello, Old Friend

Greetings, old friend.
So nice seeing you.
Let's break open some wine,
Down a brandy or two.

Sit down by the kitchen,
Watch the hours pass.
When we talk of days of old,
Holding our sides as we laugh.

I sometimes do wonder
What's happened to us?
For the kilos have piled up
And the knees constantly fuss.

Seemed just yesterday,
The wrinkles weren't old.
The body was more agile.
The bones didn't groan.

We've shared laughter through tears,
Travelled a journey of pleasure,
Endless parties guzzling wine,
Downing cocktails and liqueurs.

And late in the night,
As we talk of how time has flown,
It feels just right.
It feels just like home.

For Melvin, the young soldier

"You know, I was only eighteen", he said,
"A young man, just a child,
When my country took me to a war,
Where I had no choice but to fight.

I found myself in dirty smelly trenches,
In sodden shoes and muddy grime.
I missed my family; I was alone and scared.
My body jelly when gunfire interrupted the night.

I remember the smell; it was musty and sweet,
Of blood, tears, and sweat on my skin,
And though I was scared and exhausted,
I never stopped praying for another day to begin.

My body shivered with hunger and pain.
My young mind was numb and terrified,
For others kept losing their lives around me,
Yet I was too afraid to even cry.

I remember my chest so heavy,
The many nights when my heart was remembering,
My comrade who had fought beside me,
Lying still, his face grey and bleeding,

And how I would clutch onto my rifle,
My eyes squinting away from the scorching sun,
Stealing a glance at his lifeless body,
Whilst the rumbling grew louder in the distance.

Many countries drank champagne when the war was over,
But all I yearned for was a silent life,
Just to cherish the peace, to be alone
With my blood-red dreams and my cries.

To learn again the beauty of rustling trees,
Sitting quietly with the view from my veranda,
Watching the freedom of birds in a vast uncluttered sky,
To be myself, to hear the news, to breathe in the weather.

I still wonder about many things from the past,
If mankind has regretted their mistakes,
And it pains me so much to realise
That the scars I bear are in vain

For the enemies we fought are now our comrades,
Our allies have now become our foes.
Amongst the bitter chaos of the world, tears are forgotten.
And I ask myself, what was it all for?"

The Window Seat

Dancing above the clouds,
I catch a glimpse of heaven.
Softly I shall tread.
Gently I shall balance.
Soaring above the skies,
I am finally one with my soul.
For I see
Endless miles of happiness,
I shall one day grasp,
I will someday hold.

Chance Meeting

I caught a glimpse
As you were passing by.
And everything blurred into a moment
Of you and I.
Our eyes connected with
An uncomfortable familiarity.
As something stirred within
In my distant memory.
My feet continued walking,
Acutely aware
There was an inner churning
Of trying not to care.
But as I caught your grin,
I felt fuzzy; Then you smiled.
And time stood still,
Just for a little while.

The Tightrope

I long to walk a tightrope to overcome a dread
Of looking down from high above,
To fearlessly tread,

To wonder at the smallness of the insignificant life below.
For if I can learn from curious birds above,
Perhaps my courage will grow.

I yearn to spread my wings with no ties to bind me down,
To smell fresh air, to feel the dew
Whilst high above the ground.

But as I step on gingerly, all that I can see
Is excitement replaced by a darkness,
Of a rope unravelling mercilessly.

I am desperate to find an equilibrium, trying to ignore my paralysing fear
As I attempt to balance, not looking at
The abyss that has suddenly appeared.

I pull myself back, looking down, at the unknown majestic gorge,
Where meandering peaceful flowing streams,
Make serene journeys as I watch.

But again, illusions of a stumble, become recurring visions that I dread.
Fraying threads and endless falls,
This becomes a nightmare that does not end.

I startle, my body sweating; for this turmoil will not leave,
My heart is pounding, and I can no longer tell
If I am awake or if this is a dream.

Butterfly Moments

Her tiny hands reached gently
Towards a movement in the leaves.
A softness landed on her finger,
Fluttering ever-so cautiously.

The little creature held her curious glance
As fairy dust sprinkled from the sky,
And in that magical moment
Tiny wings and little fingers intertwined.

Delicate movements danced in the shadows,
Playing in the setting sun,
Until minutes turned into hours
And darkness turned into dawn,

And when sunshine peeped through the clouds
She kissed her little friend goodbye,
Holding on to her precious memory,
Farewelling the story of that one night.

The years passed ever-so slowly,
From many sunsets into a lifetime of days,
An ocean of butterfly moments,
Surrounding her as the world rapidly changed,

Every horizon waited patiently
For another tomorrow to unfold,
And in no time, the little girl was no longer
The mirror reflecting a woman weathered and old.

Who clutched onto her book of memories,
Her silver hair framing journeys she had tread.
Footsteps in the passage of time.
Unravelling slowly like a ball of thread.

Her fortune in life was of love,
Her hardships were never fought alone
But her heart trembled at the thought of what lay ahead,
A journey she would soon have to face on her own.

Where light would gradually begin to fade,
And her weakened body would start to let go
When a strange coldness would befall her,
One she had never known.

When out of the corner of her eye, she caught a glimpse,
Shiny and golden like the sun,
A familiar fluttering comforting her.
In that moment two hearts reached out to become one.

Once again, she was a little girl, from before,
Mesmerised by what she saw,
Her present colliding with her past
As if she had opened a mystical door.

To a hundred million moments,
Each one waiting for her to arrive
To dance with every melody,
Every symphony in her life.

A calm serenity washed over her,
As a shower of sparkles fell once more from the sky,
Lighting up the darkness before her
As her loved ones waited for her last goodbye.

And when her time finally arrived,
Beckoning her from the world she had known,
There was a gentle smile as she closed her eyes,
Holding onto the little butterfly in her soul.

The Human Race

I was surrounded by a frenzied crowd in a frantic marathon.
Their addiction became my obsession,
An impossible compulsion to run.
But my limbs soon turned heavy; my body started to cry.
As I stumbled and pushed on in pursuit
of this common finishing line,

The crowds cheered me on, urging me to run.
I became wearier.
My mind turned foggy and dull,
When in the distance I heard a sound,
The sweetest melody.
As I strained to listen,
The air filled with an incense
Of the most beautiful symphony.

I stopped in my tracks
with a realisation that I ached for more
For my race no longer mattered to me
as it did before.
I closed my eyes, and I was floating
as the music stilled my restless soul
And I finally understood
The beauty of life, the true joys to behold.

My Feathered Friend

On the gentle swaying of an aged branch
The leaves are fluttering in a rhythmic dance.
The pale sky beyond is cloudless, untouched.
As I pay attention to a glimpse caught by chance.

Of a soft fluffiness, flecks of white and brown,
A quizzical look under a feathered crown.
I watch in the quiet and hold my breath.
Whilst she taps loudly on the glass, I can see she is not afraid.

My silence is now interrupted
By the conversations of her
As she perches outside,
Curiously looking into my world.

The Day After

You are a tremble of a million sensations,
A fear I cannot explain,
A softness I can never hold,
You are my every new day.

I stumble with each step,
Dreading each farewell.
Travelling a roller coaster,
I am intoxicated, scared, content.

But you will always be my unknown,
A world I shall not exchange,
A forever bittersweet reminder that
I will never see the same day again.

My Perfect Creation

And to think that all of you
Was a tiny desire in my mind?
A blurry faded picture
that I had longed to find,

When out of the blue,
It took shape when you were born,
Looking transparent and so delicate,
The thread of life you adorned.

Patterns started to weave
An intricate picture of their own,
And a richness unfolded
Into a softness I could hold.

You reflected so many changes
Right before my very eyes,
An extraordinary image
Hidden amongst so many different lights,

When one day the perfect you appeared,
Giving me so much love
From the kaleidoscope of colour
That was running through your blood.

You were vivacious and enchanting.
For hours, I would stare.
As your image began to emerge,
You were a priceless vintage, so rare,

A woven complex tapestry,
Seen from near and afar,
An exquisite creation
Of the woman that you are.

And as your hidden beauty unravelled
Like your long and silken hair,
I was forever grateful
For every moment we would share.

The Canvas

You make your memories immortal.
With a gentle stroke of a brush.
Unravelling stories
In shades of light and dark,
Your fingers deftly working,
On the passages of your life
Racing through corridors
Against the wrinkles of time.
The rainbow swirls of colour
Are mesmerising from a distance,
Leading you away
From a complicated existence
Towards watercolours and oils,
A canvas of serenity.
This is the moment you embrace,
A temporary escape from the insanity.

My Favourite Quilt

Under your softness
Is a place where I can hide,
Curled up in your warmth.
Awaiting daylight,
Silent and safe,
I embrace your every layer
Hugging me as I curl up
For another five minutes together.

The Closed Door

The makeup comes off
And an ugliness shows.
As the surrounding walls
Watch helplessly once more.

The voice gets louder,
Amidst the smell of cologne,
A piercing quietness follows
But you already know.

Steely eyes appear
And soon the sound of shattered glass,
Soft whimpers praying
For this moment to pass.

You pick up the pieces,
As blood drips onto the floor.
How much you yearn to be
On the other side of the door.

Janus

I sense your discomfort
Oozing out from every pore,
Pretending,
Yet whispering behind closed doors.

Your conservative fabric
Denies my acceptance,
Exposing a pattern,
Regressing my existence.

Whist the modern universe
Moves forward towards a galaxy
Fighting a justice
For race, gender, and sexuality.

The worst of you is still out there,
Professing alliance to those like me,
But secretly humiliating
With your version of litany.

'Love thy neighbour as thyself,' you say,
Your public prayer every day,
But isn't what you really mean,
'Love your neighbour unless they are gay?'.

I'm tired of your scorn,
Saddened by murmurings behind my back,
Disappointed with your reflection,
Ashamed by your words of prayer.

As you continue your spiritual lessons
Professing compassion to all but a few,
All you want is to collect brownie points,
To enter a heaven for the likes of you.

31

Holding My Hand

You know my every word,
Bitter and unkind,
Every hidden behaviour
Of my cluttered mind,
The eccentricity
Of the true and inner me,
The part that makes no sense,
Only you have seen.

You have seen my nakedness
With no veil to cover my shame.
Only you know the true person
Who hides behind my name.
I question myself over,
That despite all that you have seen.
How you could still hold my hand,
And keep on loving me.

A Minute of Pleasure

My taste buds are awoken
By the scent of roasted beans.
I see dark and light swirls
As the bitterness escapes the sweet.

A wafting aroma and
An alluring spiral of smoke
Greet me from my age-old mug,
Taking me back home.

My past rushes before me,
My future is a blur.
I have travelled the fast train,
But it has made a stop here.

My mind becomes still
As I sit alone and embrace,
This beautiful moment
Whilst I sip and I taste.

I close my eyes for now
And bask in the rich flavour,
Savouring what really matters:
The now, not the later.

The Hamster

Like a hamster you run, on this blasted wheel.
Over and over searching for nothing real.
Your vision is obscured by a monotonous path,
Totally ignorant of a parallel life whizzing past.

Your energy is sapped; you start to complain.
Yet continue, exhausted by the mundane.
The wheel has such power to entice, to coax.
I ask myself, are your dreams real or just a hoax?

For there is no destination;
You just keep running blind,
A slave to meaningless possessions
whilst the second hand unwinds.

The Lion Nation

You rose up from the ashes
Of a thirty-year-old war,
Crushed, yet held your head above
Vicious waves that destroyed your shore.

You survived the wrath of militants,
Massacres in the month of prayer,
But you are now bleeding badly
And your people cry in despair.

The pearl of the Indian Ocean,
The beautiful gem that sparkled in the sea,
Is now hidden deep under a rubble,
Destroyed slowly, callously.

By leaders who were chosen
But chose to feed their own.
And now mothers and children starve in villages,
Struggling to survive the unknown.

You are haemorrhaging.
You cling onto life at death's door.
Your people, their anger
Is palpable and raw.

They wish longingly for the land
Who never did ask for much
Where once there was time for a smile
Even when life got too tough.

But now all they can do
Is to hold their heads as they watch.
The wounds growing deeper and wider,
Asking their leaders,
"Haven't you done enough?"

Is this the legacy of one?
Or arrogant gluttonous fools
Disguised as people of power
Who have led a country to ruin?

What is left are conversations,
Of desperate solutions from desperate minds.
But no one admits responsibility,
For the precious lives that have been undermined.

A country is left with almost nothing,
Her people like animals in a den
Where the rodents will start to devour
Amongst hope this will miraculously end.

But this is a nation,
That has survived many walls of flames,
And no matter how hard or how long it takes,
The Lion will rise up once again.

The Flaw of Perfection

My mind turned blank; I was lost for words.
Everything was a jumble; my thoughts remained a blur.
The images were in abundance, but my confidence was low
For I was aiming for perfection and the words just wouldn't flow.

I wondered, as I grappled with my writer's block,
My brain was now a stranger to me, forcing out only empty thoughts.
It took me time to realise that I was creating my own plight,
For I was placing unnecessary pressure on myself to get things right.

The focus on perfection was becoming a stressful game
To be better than the best, to fear judgement, to avoid shame.
Then suddenly I had an epiphany of all the happy souls who cared least of all,
Who enjoyed their every moment and laughed away their flaws.

Their presentations were not perfect, their meals were not of exquisite taste.
They would improvise if they forgot an ingredient, for they knew to play the long game.
They would ignore uneven wrapping; they would not gasp if ribbons didn't match.
For wasn't the point of the present the laughter, the surprise when it was unwrapped?

I found myself rambling, suddenly pitying those who judged and stared,
Unable to understand the freedom of wearing mismatched socks without
a care.
After all, the world had bigger problems than false sophistication and
etiquette,
Or the perfect itinerary, the perfect holiday, the perfect poem for me
to create.

And as I looked down, I was overwhelmed with utter disbelief,
For there was so much I had written faster than I could possibly read.
The poetry, it was flowing, the words had come so easily,
All because I had surrendered the pressure on myself to succeed.

The Storm

I wake up to windows rattling
And a sudden heavy crashing sound
Of wild winds howling outside like a madness
As if an ugliness has been aroused.
In the distant blackness I see
A second of brightness, a flash of light,
Fierce growling getting louder
As if a vicious animal lurks in the night.
Shapeless shadows start to follow me
And I shut my eyes in vain
To become tiny and invisible
In the madness of this pelting rain.

Lying Eyes

Your eyes somehow looked different,
Your smile was no longer yours.
Your words babbled but they meant nothing.
I didn't know you anymore.

In that moment you were someone else
Intruding into my space.
I backed away from your glance,
Still doubting my instinct, casting aside my faith,

For I once had a promise,
Of a friendship with no lies,
But what I saw now was rubble,
Nothing left to recognise.

And as you stood before me,
All that I could see,
Was an abyss of darkness
Amongst a hundred memories.

A reflection in your face,
Of a fool who had denied
To see through your excuses,
To see through your lying eyes.

Incense

Scent of a candle before me
Takes me to places I've never been,
The incense of markets in Morocco,
Or the smoky ash of ancient ruins.

Sweetness of a frangipani garden,
In a beautiful country once known as Ceylon,
Or wild rose petals floating gentle in the wind,
The most ancient flower of all.

I visit bustling streets of Vietnam
And smell fragrance of fresh lemongrass
Or the camphor of wild lavender,
In the farms of Provence.

The scent of the candle before me,
Allows me to wander free,
As I close my eyes and open my mind,
Excited for what I may see.

(Matthew 6:3-4)

Like peacocks basking,
This breed preens their bright and fluffy feathers,
Forgetting the ground, they walk on
Is the humble soil of others,

Blowing their own trumpet loudly,
To all and sundry,
Oblivious to the generous others
Who give ever-so silently.

Same Sky

You and I, we live under the same sky,
Watching headlines splashed across our screens,
Images of explosions and heavy artillery,
Sounds of ordinary people, their horrendous screams.
With eyes glued, we sit quietly,
Digesting as history unfolds,
Watching David fight Goliath.
Miles from our doorsteps, we listen to stories told.

Of how a beautiful country
Has become an eerie atmosphere of death
At the hands of a powerful megalomaniac.
We watch silently and we wait,
Whilst heavy rumbling of tanks encroaches,
In slow military precision, they surround.
Helpless mothers try to quieten their children.
Amidst the dusty bloodied lying on the ground.

Our TVs are still blaring,
Whilst news reaches millions everywhere.
And though we are so far away from this war,
It is just a click of a button that gets us back there.
And as we become silent voyeurs of this unrest,
Peeping at one man destroying mankind,
In the comfort and safety of our armchairs,
We forget we all live under the same sky.

Our Favourite Place

Snatching time
In a familiar place,
It's always the same.
They all know our face.

Warm smiles greet us,
"How is everyone today?"
Our mouths are watering
"I'll have the medium-rare steak."

"How about the chilli crust pizza,
Ribs, or mac and cheese?"
Or "What the hell, we'll indulge.
Half a dozen oysters, please!"

Heads tipping back,
The food brings us together.
It feels just like home,
Just tastes so much better.

Picture Imperfect

You feign a perfect façade,
Hiding the naked truth,
Portraying a magic
Of the digital world you choose.

Pristine smiles manufactured,
A filtered light, your best friend
For the world to see a beauty,
Until the cinematography ends.

The best images are exposed,
Allowing voyeurs into a gilded frame.
Where a show of classy sophistication
Displays the mastery of a skilful game.

A reel of eternal happiness,
Which stops abruptly behind closed doors?
Where a manufactured Garden of Eden,
Displays a life which was never really yours.

Men in White

I am watching miniature men,
Battleships in the green.
The mortal combat starts. My mind jumbles,
For I don't know what this means.
I hear mobs yelling;
My heart skips a beat.
Someone shouts "Over!",
But it's never over in this morbid heat.

And from a distance
I hear a loud "Appeal!"
Whilst rabid masses jump up in synchrony,
It's quite surreal.
I feel stuck in a time warp,
Looping over and over again,
Of men in white, two bats and a ball
And an insanity unfolding on a grassy terrain.

Goodbye

I rest my body next to you,
Gently stroking your head,
The peaceful silence rudely disturbed
By cold machines beside your bed.

I feel your weak heart beating.
Your face is cool next to mine.
As I watch your body heaving
Heavily one more time.

I cling onto you and look away
For I don't want you to see me cry.
I whisper into your ear,
"It's ok; I'll be alright."

I see a teardrop glisten
From the corner of your eye,
And I know that you have heard me.
I cannot bring myself to say, "Goodbye."

And as I watch you slowly leave my world,
I try hard to hold on forever,
For I know too soon, you and I will be just a memory.
And this will be our very last time together.

The Dreamer

Never did I imagine another just like me,
Dreaming in a world entwining thoughts with imagery,
Walking down familiar roads, the view never the same,
Grasping at new wonders, different pictures in a frame.

Your mind, your constant companion, journeys deep into your thoughts,
Fleeting in the moment, captured lest they will be lost.
Whilst all those around you, they just carry on,
Your visions and your memories take you places never before.

A day's travel journey is so many miles ahead.
You share the meandering dreams of excitement sprinkled with dread.
Feelings, they direct you, so your freedom is no longer caged.
Fantasies are welcome and reality avenged.

A world of different colours, the words a stranger said.
The passages of walking souls, you wonder where their lives have led,
When suddenly an image springs up for just a little while
Or a dark and brooding look lights up to reveal a handsome smile.

I wish someone had told me, "Remember you are you,
Different from the others, for their goals they must pursue.
So, when they hurry incessantly, missing all the views around,
You will have a million pictures and endless dreams abound.

The dreams will be assuring, happy thoughts through shades of fear,
And amidst a future alluring, a contentment will appear.
The dreams will give you meaning, wisdom in a pearl,
An escape from reality in a superfluous world."

Never did I imagine another just like me
Until I saw your quiet need of silence and serenity
To allow your dreams to wonder with no knocking on the door,
With no boundaries to surrender, where your dreams are only yours.

July 1983

Fire and smoking cinders, it was a Sunday in July.
Bloodstains splattered on a portrait right before my younger eyes.
Strong smells of sweat and petrol pervaded,
A foreboding sky,
Heartbeats trembled and I saw a fear, as I kept asking myself why.

Matches and kerosene became possessions of heartless animal mobs,
Ravaging feverishly like demons possessed, ransacking homes, looting shops.
Dark grey ashes floated high above to warn those escaping homes.
Imminent danger followed plumes of smoke; life no longer theirs to own.

The politicians and the military chose to look the other way that day,
Applauding instead the horrific genocide whilst beasts entertained for another day.
And sanctimonious yellow robes worshipped prejudice and demonic hatred,
Discarding doctrine for Molotov cocktails,
Remorseless for the divide they created.

Ruthless masses surrounded property, playing roulette with human fate.
Their victims, eyes blank in terror, all they could only do, was to wait.
As evil crowds of hungry people watched their victims being set alight,
Dousing them in gasoline whilst they cried, begging for their lives.

Some were trapped, helpless and terrified, whilst their murderers' jostled cars.
Axes and machetes were all they could see through shattered window glass.
Many were locked in fleeing vehicles, hunted with no chance to survive.
How could I forget the glimpse of that woman, the pure horror in her eyes?

The sacred symbol on her forehead, was hastily wiped away with tears,
For those who were once friends and strangers, now were persons she feared.
Innocence was handcuffed unjustly, that week in July.
So how can you ask me to salute the gracious beauty,
Whilst I still hear their haunting cries?

The mountains, seas, and friendly faces still camouflage stories of a sinister past,
Where dark bigotry still exists, hidden so deep, though much time has passed.
In a country and her people where there should be much shame and regret
We choose to justify, forget,
Blame others instead.

The Passing Ship

The ship sailed her journey,
Travelling a thousand miles,
Navigating an infinite ocean
Of rising and falling tides,
Joyous waves were bobbing over,
But the turbulence was deep below,
And gradually a weariness overwhelmed her.
She found herself steering towards an unknown.

A fearful disorientation took over,
As the sea of blackness started to surround.
And soon a dangerous comfort of oblivion,
Began to persuade her it was easier to drown.
Afar the light of a beacon
Began to draw closer, shining bright.
Soon the sturdy vessel moored beside her
In that dark and misty night.

It convinced her heavy subconscious,
To leave the swirling that consumed,
Offering her a safe passage towards the helm,
And leading her gently towards the view
Of the magnificent horizon ahead
Lined by a thousand tiny twinkling lights,
Beckoning, guiding, encouraging her
To continue the voyage into the night.

And as she caught a glimpse
Of the majestic glorious sunrise,
Arising out of the midnight gloom,
Her salty tears began to dry.
She had been given a newfound strength
To travel the infinite waters just once more.
Her journey seemed somehow less weary,
Her burden lighter than before,

And she realised no matter how vast the ocean,
No matter how tides would fall or rise,
Nor how far the distance,
She had learned something she could never deny.
And from then on, amidst any darkness,
She would remember that one fateful night,
Of the compassion from the passing ship,
That chose to shine her a light.

Our Children

Why do we ignore our smallness
Choosing instead to become
A world of warring nations
When we should fight as one?
Why do we brush aside,
Our lasting legacy,
Of raging floods, hunger,
destruction and disease?

Harsh winters. Scorching summers
A cold intelligence, an unimaginable terrain,
A world where our children will have to endure
Freedom in chains
Our eyes remain wide shut.
To the truth that remains,
Our selfish selves knowing, we will be long gone
By the time we get the blame.

For My Patient

As I walked the familiar corridor, I called you by your name.
My feet were dragging, a mask hiding my pain.
And as you turned to look at me, I saw the clenching of your hands.
The sleepless night you'd had the night before
From the hope you yearned to have.

And as I called your name once more,
You watched the expression on my face,
Searching for a little clue, a tiny hope you could embrace.
I thought of how I would convey this cruelty to you
Yet say the words in a way to give hope and optimism too.

It seemed a long walk into my room,
The walls seemed so bare.
And as you slowed your pace yet once again, I knew you were aware.
For by the time, you sat down in the sterile leather chair,
I watched you look straight at me, your eyes in full despair.

And as I gently spoke to you,
It was not the news that you had hoped.
I could feel your stomach churning; I could feel you felt alone.
And everything else I uttered I knew it was in vain.
For your life had just come crumbling down there was nothing left but pain.

And I tried so hard to do my best,
To give honestly, to give you hope,
Not to exaggerate nor to minimise, just enough to help you cope.
I tried to answer your every question, to be truthful as I spoke,
But never once did you ask the one question you feared most.

And my heart shattered watching you
As you tried to pretend to me
What I knew was a strong façade, hiding the trembling underneath.
And as you slowly turned to leave, I watched you try to hold yourself together,
For the life you once knew was gone.
And your sadness would now live inside of me forever.

Last Words

And so is this it when my life finally unfolds,
The mind stuck at eighteen, bones withered and old?
What have I learned from my time on this Earth?
Have I just existed, or given back to our world?

Have I offered my hand and steadied a fall,
Or walked on regardless, pretending nothing was wrong?
Have I knocked people over to become first in the race,
Looking smugly at those struggling at slow pace?

Have I stood up in anger against those who did not care,
Calling out bigotry, or have I just sat quietly and stared?
Have I learned, have I learned, have I learned nothing at all,
That for brightness to follow, darkness must fall?

And that true love exists not only in fairy tales?
That time is a luxury we forget time again?
Have I stood high on a podium, raised my hand to the clouds
Or lived for applause from those shallow crowds?

Collecting titles and silver,
A castle, a crown,
Forgetting nothing is ours,
When we are one with the ground?

The End

And so, her master's words finally unfolded.
Into a work of art.
The little girl no longer saw his creation.
As an arduous task.

And from that day
Whenever craziness churned within,
She would close her eyes and dream of the
"Golden dancing daffodils"

For a tiny fire had been set alight,
A flame growing slowly, into a yearning inside
To pen her stories into a verse, into a rhyme,
Capturing her ocean of butterfly moments,
lest they be lost in time.

Gratitude

Writing poetry has allowed me to open a door to a very special place. It took me over 4 years to gather courage to share the first of my collection and for this I am grateful to so many.

Firstly, to my parents Keerthi and Tilak Mendis who gave me the precious gifts of learning, opportunity, wisdom and love. My thanks will never be enough.

To my husband and my children, you are my world. Upul, this book is my gift to you. You are the constant in my everchanging universe. Thank you for always holding my hand.

To Amil and Anisha, who have shown me the importance of pursuing dreams and believing. I am eternally grateful to be your mum. A special thank you to Anisha for helping me with my book cover.

To my family in Singapore and Sri Lanka, who have taught me that the bonds of love will remain strong, no matter the circumstance nor the distance.

To Anouke and Praha, for walking beside me always and to Matty for his quiet solidarity and the delightful challenge to write 'Our favourite place.'

To my closest girlfriends, you know who you are, for many priceless moments over the years.

To Tellwell support who took away my fear of self-publishing by making the process seamless.

And finally, to my teachers, colleagues and patients, thank you. Because of you, I am able to fulfil a longing to keep giving back to the world in a small but meaningful way.

About the Author

The author is a family medical practitioner who enjoys a quiet life in the leafy outer suburbs of Sydney. She treasures her time with her husband, her two children and close friends.

As a child, her mother introduced her to the wonderful world of poetry, a gift that has become a place of refuge where she feels free to express her thoughts.

Her journey of life has taken her across three countries, from her land of birth, Singapore, to Sri Lanka and finally to Australia. Her experiences during this time are reflected in her first collection of poetry.

Made in the USA
Las Vegas, NV
03 July 2024

91824357R00049